Gypsy Swing & Hot Club Rh
for Guitar

by Dix Bruce

• Learn melodies & chord progressions to 12 great Gypsy Swing standards in the style recorded by Django Reinhardt, Stephane Grappelli and the Quintette of the Hot Club of France

• Learn moveable closed position swing/jazz chords

• Learn the swing guitar rhythm comp

• Jam along with a great "Hot Club"-style rhythm section

• Practice rhythm and soloing by playing along. *We'll jam all night long!*

• Music includes standard notation, guitar tablature, chords, lyrics

MUSIX

P.O. Box 231005, Pleasant Hill, CA 94523
www. musixnow.com

901 BCD

Cover design by Charlotte Gibb. Back cover photo of Dix Bruce by Theresa Hioki.
Thanks to Bob Bergman for his most helpful suggestions.

Musix, PO Box 231005, Pleasant Hill, CA 94523 • www.musixnow.com

Contents

Introduction to Gypsy Swing

The music of the Quintette of the Hot Club of France with Django Reinhardt on guitar and Stephane Grappelli on violin is a kind of mystic holy grail for fans of string swing and jazz. Django and Stephane played with exceptional virtuosity, passion, excitement, and a life force that's still infectious over fifty years after they played their last notes together. The sound is, at times, unbelievable. How could human beings play with such precision and fire? And their music swings! When you hear it, you want to play along!

The purpose of this book and CD set is to get you started playing music in the Gypsy Swing and Hot Club style. You'll first learn "swing" chords and Hot Club-style rhythm playing on twelve great songs, most of which Django Reinhardt and Stephane Grappelli recorded. Then you can concentrate on the melodies and practice playing along with the recorded band. Finally, you'll develop your own solos and practice them with the band that never gets tired! In addition to having a lot of fun, you'll build a repertoire of songs, chords, chord progressions, melodies, and leads.

Start by reading the music in the book and playing along with the recorded rhythm sections, first at a slow speed with just guitar accompaniment, then, when you're ready, with a full blown "Hot Club"-style band. The band will play through each tune several times to give you the opportunity to practice rhythm chords and melodies and your own solo improvisations. It's just like having your own "Hot Club" band on call. You can work on a tune, solo, or passage for hours, perfecting it without wearing out your fellow players. The opportunities for advancing your reading and improvising skills while expanding your repertoire are unlimited. ***We'll jam all night long!***

Most of the songs and chord progressions in the book and on the CD were recorded by Django Reinhardt and Stephane Grappelli and are important standards both in the Gypsy Swing world and in the larger world of Swing & Jazz. The music includes standard notation, tablature, chords, lyrics, chord diagrams, and suggested fingerings.

For the most part, the songs are presented in the keys the Hot Club played them in. There are exceptions and I took some liberties here and there for the sake of variety and harmonic interest. One of my goals with this project is to help make keys interchangeable to you and prepare you to play any song in any key with ease. Learning closed position chords and melodies will give you a great head start. You will snicker at songs written in five sharps, laugh out loud at four flats! Download my Scale and Chord Chart for reference. It shows all the major scales and chords for every key. It's a great tool for transposing. Go to the "Downloads" section of my web site: www.musixnow.com.

Measure numbers are shown beginning with the second staff of each song on the left side above the treble clef sign. I often refer to these numbers in the text accompanying the songs. Numbering starts after any pickup measures.

Melodies and rhythm section backups to all the tunes in this book are on the recording at slow and regular speeds. First you'll hear a melody played on guitar slowly, with just guitar backup. Then you'll hear the same melody at regular speed, with the full band. Finally you'll hear the band playing the song from beginning to end, several times through, without any recorded lead. You'll play all the chords, melodies, solos and improvisations!

Most melodies are written with no open string notes. Likewise all chords are shown in closed position with no open strings. Beginning and intermediate guitarists tend to perceive melodies or chords with open string notes as somehow easier than those with all closed position or fretted notes. That may be because melodies or chords with open string notes are more familiar than those with all closed position notes. However, there's a great advantage to knowing chords and melodies in closed positions. Closed position chords and entire chord progressions as well as melodies and solos can be easily moved up and down the fingerboard to new positions and keys. Suppose you learn "Avalon" as written in the key of F. Great, as long as the people you play with perform it in the same key. You might come across a tenor sax player who wants to perform the song in the key of Ab. If you know the chord progression or melody in a closed position, you simply move everything up three frets. The small numbers between the lyric and tablature lines are suggested fretting finger numbers for melodies. If you can't reach the notes with these fingers, feel free to change them. Chord diagrams include the same information and are explained further in the "Swing Rhythm Guitar" section on page 7.

The recorded backup band plays in the style of the Quintette of the Hot Club of France and includes me, Dix Bruce, on rhythm guitar; Jason Vanderford on rhythm guitar; and Steve Hanson on string bass. I also play the guitar leads. Tuning tones are on track one of the CD. Let's get started!

Photo by Kathi Bruce

l. to r.: Jason Vanderford, Steve Hanson, Dix Bruce.

How to work with the book and CD

• **Before you dive into a chord progression or melody, read along as you first listen to the recording.** It's a good idea to review the chords and scales of the key each song is in, especially if you are not used to playing in that key. Learn the chords and chord progressions by playing along with the slow version first. Gradually work your way up to the regular speed band version. If you're new to this style of music, there will be a lot to learn: chord positions, the rhythm comp, and the melody — not to mention any solos you develop or improvise.

• **When you've memorized the chords and the chord progression, try the melody,** again mastering the slow version before you move on to the full speed band version. Then try moving the melody up or down an octave, whatever the instrument allows. Also try moving melodies to other keys. If the melody includes open string notes, find their fretted equivalents and transpose these melodies too.

• **Once you can play the melody along with the band, try making up your own solos.** Start by changing the memorized melodies slightly as you play along to make them swing more than the versions on the printed page. By "rhythmizing" a given melody you can create an entirely new solo. I demonstrate this technique on several of the songs including "After You've Gone" on page 16 and "Chicago" on page 23. Be sure to try transposing the melody up or down an octave from where it's written. We'll work through that on "The Sheik of Araby" on page 10. Play these exercises again and again until you have something that feels like your own solo. Remember, the recorded band will back you up for hours with no complaints as you try this melody or that lick. It's a good idea to write out your improvisations and keep them in a spiral bound music notebook. That way you can refer back and revise them as you progress. Work with the slow recording of a song until you're ready for the full speed band version. You can isolate the lead or rhythm part from either version by simply adjusting the balance control on your stereo. If you're listening with headphones you can take one side off.

• **Listen to how guitarists and other musicians that you admire play these songs and how they solo on them.** The most obvious place to start is with the masters: Django Reinhardtand Stephane Grappelli. Listen closely and try to analyze how they approach a melody or chord progression. Be encouraged to "borrow" from Django, Stephane, or other masters. Learn their vocabularies and how they assemble phrases into a coherent whole. Learning to improvise in music is a lot like learning to speak. We all have the same letters, words and phrases which we continually recycle into sentences and paragraphs that, hopefully, express what we're feeling. The goal is to build your own musical/swing vocabulary which will eventually allow you to speak through your instrument.

• **As you're listening for inspiration, don't limit yourself to guitar players.** Listen to everybody that you think is great, no matter what instrument they play. Identify what it is about a musician's playing or singing that moves you. Try to incorporate some of that into your own playing. Make yourself curious enough to listen to your favorite recorded musicians play a lick or passage until you figure it out — a hundred times if necessary.

• **Experiment with leaving the melodies completely behind you.** Sing along with the tracks and vocalize your ideas. Learn to sing what you're trying to play, even if you think you have a lousy voice. Look for new ideas and input constantly, and try to make them a part of your playing. Practice playing whatever is in your mind and heart. Don't quit working with the track after one solo — especially if it doesn't sound as good as you want right away — work it through the whole track. One of the advantages of the back up track is that you can try out an idea and play it on several solos in succession gaining control of it as you go.

• **Make the recorded band** *your* **band and work out with it daily.** The more you play, the better you'll play. You'll gain strength, stamina, and focus as you train yourself to play two, three, four or more solos in a row. A typical gig might consist of four one hour sets with fifteen minute breaks in between. Start by jamming along with the CD for ten to fifteen minutes a day and work up from there. Check out my other "play along with the band" book and CD sets: **BackUP TRAX: Swing & Jazz** (includes guitar TAB)**, BackUP TRAX: Early Jazz**

& Hot Tunes, BackUP TRAX: Basic Blues (includes guitar TAB), and **BackUP TRAX: Traditional Jazz & Dixieland**. Though **Early Jazz** and **Traditional Jazz** don't include guitar TAB, you'll still enjoy jamming along. Full details and samples are available on my web site: www.musixnow.com. If you play enough you'll eventually find that ideas and solos will begin to emerge. It's a great and rewarding process of discovery!

Author Michael Dregni wrote a very interesting biography of Django Reinhardt titled "Django: The Life and Times of a Gypsy Legend" (Oxford University Press). For more information on Stephane Grappelli, you'll love the 2-DVD release "A Life in the Jazz Century" (Music on Earth). It includes all known film footage of Django Reinhardt.

There are countless reissues of the music of the Quintette of the Hot Club of France and of Django and Stephane's recordings. Some of the best and most economical are the four and five disc sets on JSP Records. I recommend "Django Reinhardt: The Classic Early Recordings in Chronological Order" (JSPCD901), "Django Reinhardt Vol. 2: Paris and London 1937 to 1948" (JSPCD904), and "Django in Rome 1949/1950" (JSP919). Stephane Grappelli is included in all three sets. The first consists mainly of classic Hot Club material and in order to understand the music in this book, you *must* hear it. "Django in Rome 1949/1950" is interesting in that it presents Django and Stephane with a more "modern," non-Hot Club style rhythm section with piano, bass, and drums. It's all great music!

Now let's jam!

Dix Bruce (June 2007)

Photo by Theresa Hioki

Dix Bruce is a writer and award-winning musician from the San Francisco Bay Area. He has written over fifty book / CD sets and videos, mostly for Mel Bay Publications. He has also produced instructional DVDs including "Basic Swing Guitar" for Stefan grossman's Guitar Workshop. Dix has played guitar with San Francisco's Royal Society Jazz Orchestra since the late 1980s. Visit him online at www.musixnow.com.

Swing Guitar Rhythm

Swing Guitar Rhythm is a combination of two elements:

- closed position moveable chords, and
- the "comp" or pulse of the strummed closed position chords.

In many styles of music, guitar chords are strummed and the notes are allowed to ring. In swing and jazz we use closed position chords with no open string notes because we want to be able to control how long the notes of the chord ring to set up our rhythmic groove. We also want these chords to be moveable to other positions and keys. The familiar A7 below left has open string notes. If we strum it, strings one (furthest to the right), three, five and six will continue to ring even if we lift our first and third fingers after we strum the chord. The A7 on the right below is a closed position form. The number to the right of the chord diagram tells us to play this form at the fifth fret. The "x" under strings one and five tells us to mute or not play these strings. In this closed A7 form the side of my first finger mutes the fifth string, the side of my third finger mutes the first. The "r" under string six shows where the root of the form, in this case an A, is located. The name of the root changes as you move the form up and down the fingerboard and will name the chord. Muting the whole chord while strumming is accomplished by loosening the fretting hand grip just enough after the strum to stop the sound.

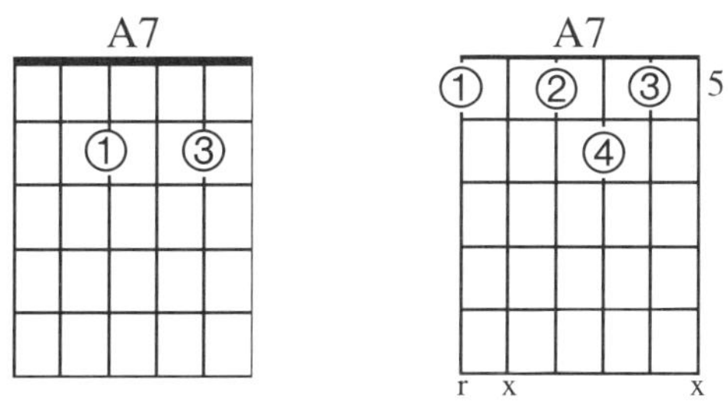

Chord diagrams are shown with the individual songs in the approximate order they appear in a progression. In some cases alternate fingerings or forms are also given. Try them all and see how each works in a particular situation. One might sound better or be easier to move in and out of than another. Try substituting other versions of the same chord from other songs in the book. Each form has a slightly different tonal color but an A7 is an A7 is an A7. For the sake of the rhythmic comp, use closed chord forms with no open string notes. Remember to swap out chords of the same quality: an A7 for an A7, an Am6 for an Am6, but not an A7 for an Am6.

The "comp" is a pattern of strumming with the picking hand and pulsing with the fretting hand to set up a groove that propels the rhythm. Let's look at 4/4 rhythm, which is the most prevalent meter in Swing and Gypsy Swing. In 4/4 we play four beats to the measure: 1 — 2 — 3 — 4. To play the comp we let strums one and three ring a bit but mute two and four after they're played. That gives the kind of "cha — chuk — cha — chuk" rhythm that Django and Stephane usually had behind them in the Quintette. According to Michael Dregni, the author of "Django: The Life and Times of a Gypsy Legend," this rhythm became known as *la pompe* or "the pump." Dregni describes it as: "striking each beat with a percussive strum, any sustain choked off by dampening the strings immediately after the downward strum." Listen to the demonstration of the comp in 4/4 and 3/4 on track two of the CD. As you listen to the full rhythm tracks, notice the difference in the way Jason Vanderford and I approach the comp. Jason's is very percussive, like Dregni describes above, almost like a snare drum, without much harmonic content. I let my strums ring a little longer and you hear the notes of the chord a bit more. I think the two styles work well together and I very much enjoyed playing with both Jason and Steve Hanson.

Avalon

"Avalon" is a popular standard from 1920. The composers are listed in the original sheet music as Al Jolson and Vincent Rose. I've always wondered if Jolson actually had a hand in composing the song or if he bought into it, which was common practice for big stars of the time.

The melody is made up primarily of half notes and played at a quick tempo. The effect is to make the accompaniment sound as if it's in double time. The four measure string bass introduction is similar to one on a recording of "Avalon" by Django Reinhardt and Stephane Grappelli with the Quintette of the Hot Club of France. Occasionally an introduction is added to a song form. In this case, the string bass plays unaccompanied, one time, at the very beginning of the tune. You, as a member of the band, need to be able to recognize where the intro ends and where the form of the song begins.

The ending we recorded is a common and fun Hot Club / traditional jazz-style ending. The band stops after an accented break on beat one of the F (or "one") chord of measure thirty one of the last chorus. After that I continue by sliding a tremoloed chord form up the fingerboard from C to F to end on a last hit with the band. See the chords below.

I added some substitute chords in parenthesis in measures nine through twelve. When the progression stays on a five dominant (V) chord, in this case a C7, for several measures, we can often swap in a two minor seven chord (ii m7), a Gm7 here. Try this alternate progression and see if you like it. You could also plug these changes in at measures one through four. Identify other extended passages of dominant seven chords in this and other songs and experiment with adding in a ii m7 chord.

By the way, the lyrics to all the songs are included. Even if you're not a singer, I think it's important to know a song by its lyrics. I often have them running in my head as I play a melody or compose a solo. It helps me stay grounded on each specific song.

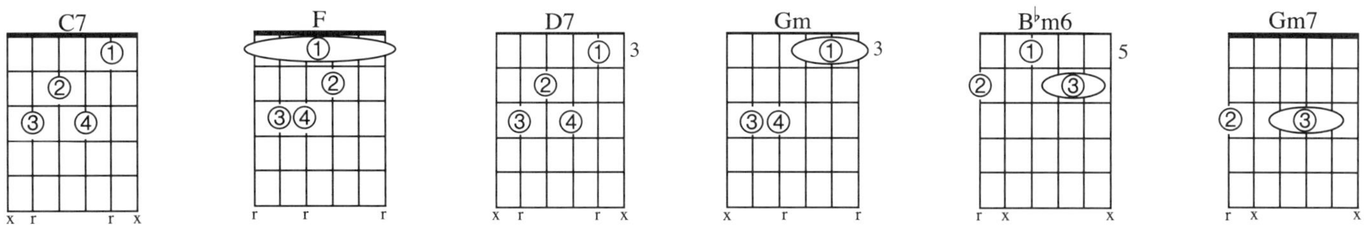

Ending chords:

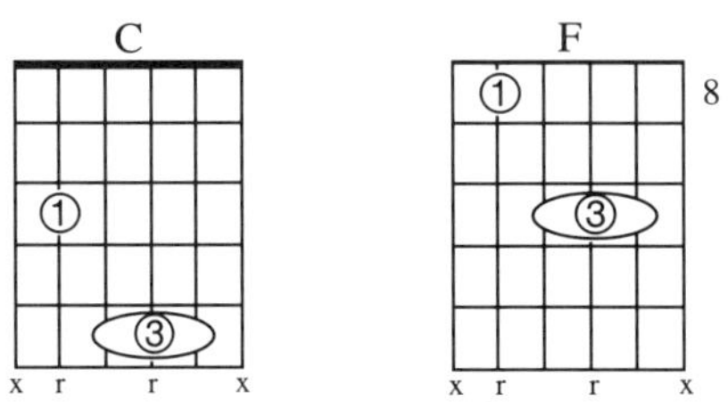

Avalon

Key of F, CD tracks 3-5 | *Jolson & Rose, 1920*

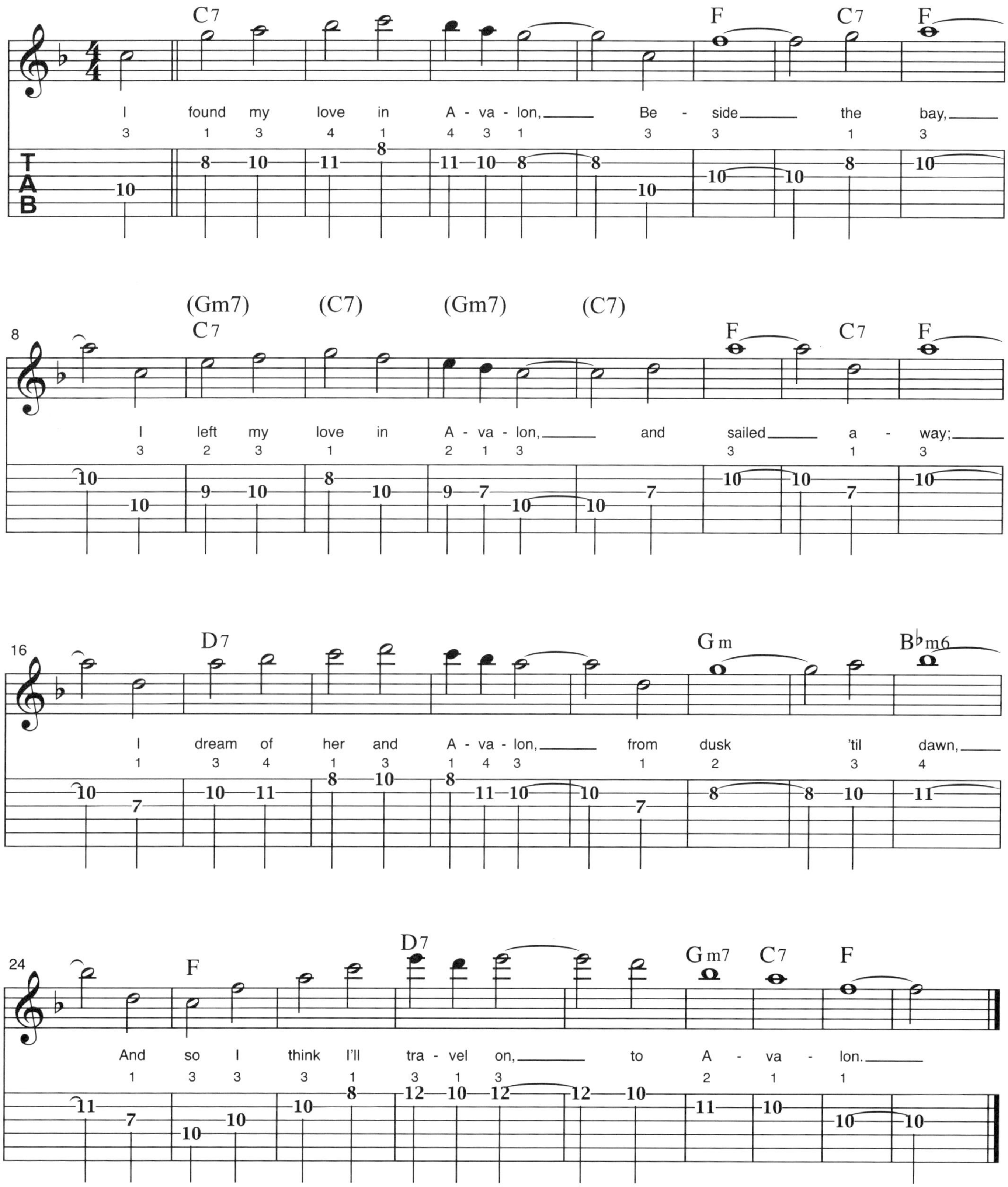

The Sheik of Araby

"The Sheik of Araby" first appeared in 1921 and has been a popular standard ever since. It's usually played in the key of Bb, which is where I've written it below. The melody is a combination of staccato and legato notes with a repetitive rhythmic motif: quarter notes followed by dotted halves.

The melody is presented in two different octaves. The first shown below is the upper octave melody played above the eighth fret. Since I thought this version might be a challenge to those of you not used to playing up the neck, you'll hear this melody on the slow recording. A second, lower octave version of "The Sheik of Araby" follows the first. This is the melody you'll hear on the up-to-speed excerpt. I'm a firm believer in the value of moving whatever you learn on the guitar up or down to as many octaves as possible. It might be a challenge for you at first, but it's a great way to get to know the fingerboard especially when you've already memorized a melody and have a pretty good idea how it goes. I suggest that you transpose every song in this book up or down as the limits of the fingerboard allow. You'll be amazed at what it will teach you about the guitar and knowing a melody in an additional octave is like having an extra solo on a song.

Like all the melodies in this book, both the high and low octave melodies to "The Sheik of Araby" are in closed position. Practice moving both up and down to other keys. For example, move the lower octave melody up two frets to the key of C. Move the upper octave melody down three frets to the key of G.

The ending is one of those "chord tremolo windup, take no prisoners, the song is over, now go home" type of things. This music is just too much fun!

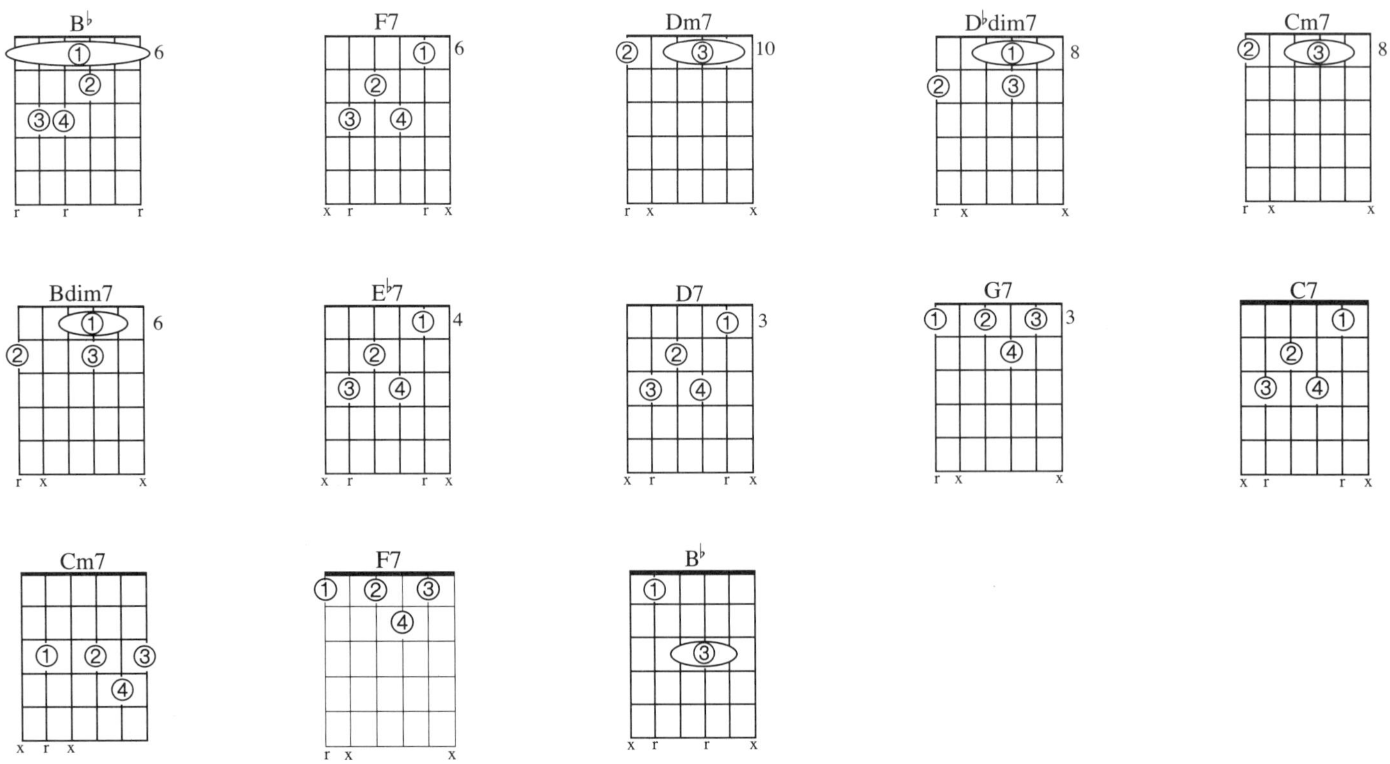

The Sheik of Araby

Key of Bb, CD tracks 6-8

T. Snyder, H. Smith, & F. Wheeler, 1921

Arrangement © 2007 by Dix Bruce • www.musixnow.com

The Sheik of Araby transposed down an octave:

Some of These Days

"Some of These Days" is a favorite of Red Hot Mama singers the world over. One of its interesting aspects is that it modulates between the keys of E minor and G major. E minor is the relative minor of G, G is the relative major of E minor and they share the same scale and key signature.

I diverge a bit here and there from the straight rhythm and add accents and counter rhythms. Django would often add little rhythmic flourishes like these behind Stephane's solos. As with everything he played, Django was a master of these rhythmic accents. When I add rhythmic variations like these I try to keep them to a minimum so they won't detract from the groove or compete with what the soloist is playing. There's always a danger of adding too much.

The melody has a lot of chromatic tones in it as you can see from all the accidentals (sharps and flats). As a result, the suggested fingerings shift around a bit and you won't always play the same note at the same fret with the same finger. If you find the given fretting finger suggestions difficult, experiment with your own positions and fingerings.

Some of These Days

Key of Em, G, CD tracks 9-11 — *Sheldon Brooks, 1910*

G
C
- ly, Just for you on - ly, For you know hon -
E7
Am
- ey, You've had your way, And when you leave
C
C♯dim7
G
E7
me, You know it'll grieve me; I'll miss my little
A7
D7
G
ba - by, Some of these days.

After You've Gone

"After You've Gone" is another great standard played by jazz musicians *everywhere*! It's a bit unusual in that the first chord of measure one is a IV ("four chord") in this case an F. That might lead you to conclude that the song is in the key of F when it's actually in the key of C. The foolproof way to know what key a piece is in is to look at the key signature, the space between the treble clef sign and time signature on the left hand side of the music. The number of sharps or flats will define the key.

The example above from "Avalon" has one flat in its key signature and that means that the song is in the key of F, even though the first chord is a C7. If there are no sharps or flats in the key signature, which is the case with "After You've Gone," the piece is in the key of C. For more info on the number of sharps and flats in keys, download the Scale and Chord chart from www.musixnow.com. Another fairly reliable method for determining the key of a piece is to find what chord the song ends on. If it ends on a C, the piece is probably in the key of C. If it ends on a Bb chord, then it's most likely in the key of Bb. If it ends on a Dm chord, the piece is probably in D minor. There are exceptions, but they're rare in pop and jazz.

I didn't play the up to speed melody exactly as written but added a few slides and rhythmic syncopations here and there when I recorded it. This is typical of a jazz interpretation of a melody. You can use this type of interpretation to compose melody-based solos.

We played a stop or "break" in the rhythm track at measure thirteen on the last time through. I kept a rhythm click going on the guitar to guide you. Having a break like this is a very common tool that musicians use to add interest and tension to a performance. As a player you need to be able to count the rhythm in your head and not loose the groove. This break will give you practice counting.

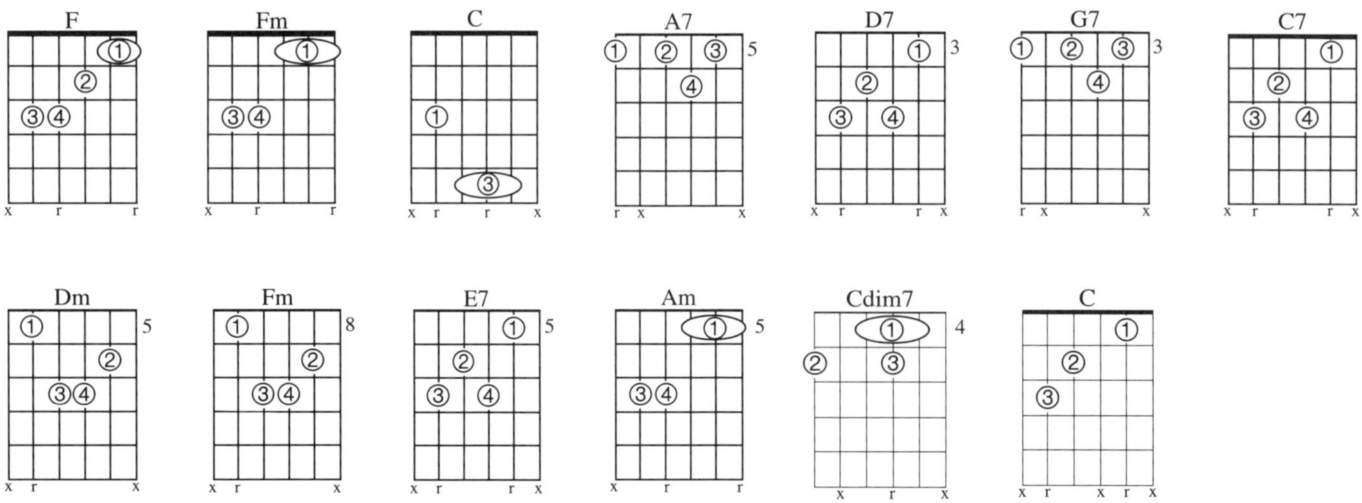

After You've Gone

Key of C, CD tracks 12-14

Creamer & Layton, 1918

Arrangement © 2007 by Dix Bruce • www.musixnow.com

Baby Won't You Please Come Home?

"Baby Won't You Please Come Home?" is in the key of Eb. If you're not used to it, playing in flat keys like Eb, Bb, Ab, etc., can strike fear into your heart. Once you've had experience playing in different keys, you'll find that one key is pretty much the same as any other. If you want to play swing and jazz, it's important that you reach that point. Different players and especially different singers, will want to perform songs in different keys. For example, a horn player might like flat keys like F, Bb, Eb, etc., or a singer may need to move "Baby Won't You Please Come Home" from Eb to the key of C or G. Since the singer can't adjust his or her range, you need to adjust what you play to where they need to sing. Be prepared! Don't shy away from keys and sets of chords that you might find initially challenging. Practice moving all the songs in this book to a variety of other keys. The Scale and Chord chart that you can download from www.musixnow.com will show you how to transpose the chords to any key.

"Baby Won't You Please Come Home" has an unusual form: it's eighteen measures in length. Most of the other songs in this book and in the jazz / pop repertoire are built on sixteen or thirty two bar forms. "Baby Won't You Please Come Home" has two additional bars that include a built in "I really mean it!" Here's where the singer drops to one knee and really sells the song. On the slow recording I play measure sixteen as written. On the up-to-speed recording I don't play the triplet. Rather I play the first four notes as eighths.

The last two measures of the last chorus of the rhythm track are extended. Instead of playing two beats each of the F7 and Bb7, we play one whole measure of each. There are several types of extended and special endings like this in Gypsy Swing and Jazz and we'll explore a few of them in this book.

Below you'll see two different forms of the F7 chord. Both will work for either F7 though each has a unique sound. Try using the form that's closest to the chords before and after to avoid an awkward hand shift. The two Ab chords are also interchangeable. It gets down to whether you like to use your thumb or not.

I added a few bass run fills in the guitar rhythm to "Baby Won't You Please Come Home?" All lead up to the root bass note of whatever chord we're playing at the time.

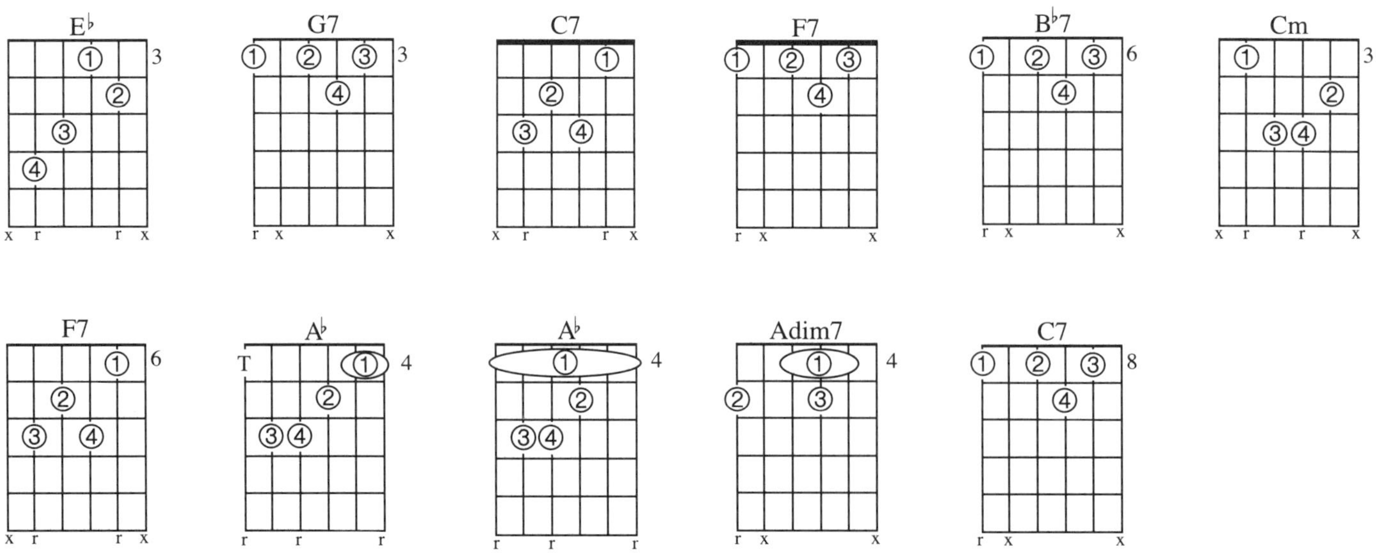

Baby Won't You Please Come Home?

Key of Eb, CD tracks 15-17 *C. Williams & C. Warfield, 1919*

Swing in Minor

"Swing in Minor" is based on a famous Django Reinhardt and Stephane Grappelli tune called "Minor Swing." Django and Stephane recorded it several times and played it in the key of Am, so that's where "Swing in Minor" is set. David Grisman recorded a wonderful arrangement of "Minor Swing" in the late 1970s in the key of Dm. Grisman's version is well known among acoustic string players. Check out the Dm version of "Swing in Minor" on page 22. Unfortunately we didn't have room for a track in Dm on the CD. You can use the melody to "Swing in Minor" in either key as a solo over the changes to "Minor Swing."

"Swing in Minor" has a somewhat unusual form with two different melodies or "heads." One is played at the beginning of the tune, one at the end. We've edited the two together on the CD so you can practice both. As you'll hear, both are punctuated by band breaks or stops with fills by the string bass. Since the band plays one whole note in every measure in the first part it is incumbent on the soloist to provide very clear swing rhythm structure and timing. I've written the melody in measure one, which repeats in measures three and five, with two different fingerings. Pick the one that works best for you. If you use the measure one fingering, you have to move your hand way up the neck to play measure two. The fingering in measure three avoids this.

I play an octave E in measure seven. Django used octaves extensively and often played whole passages or solos with them. As you fret the two notes on strings one and three, you'll need to mute the second string with your fretting hand. Here's a visual clue to find where octaves are located on the fingerboard: to play octaves on strings one and three or two and four, the upper note is separated from the lower note by two open frets and one string. To play octaves on strings three and five or four and six, the upper note is separated from the lower note by one open fret and one string. We'll do more work with octaves in "China Boy" on page 26.

The last four measures of the out head are pitched quite high on the fingerboard. If you're playing a guitar without a cutaway, you might want to move this passage down an octave. The music is below. For practice, try moving both heads down an octave.

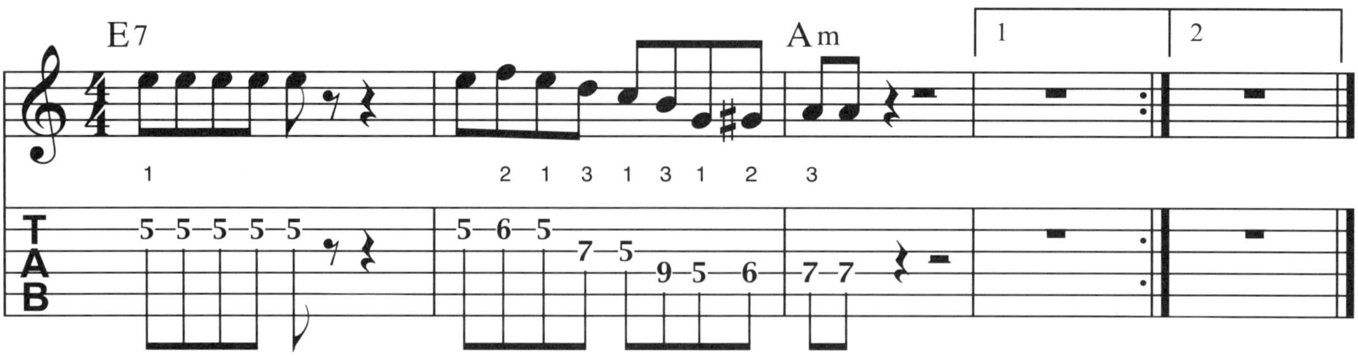

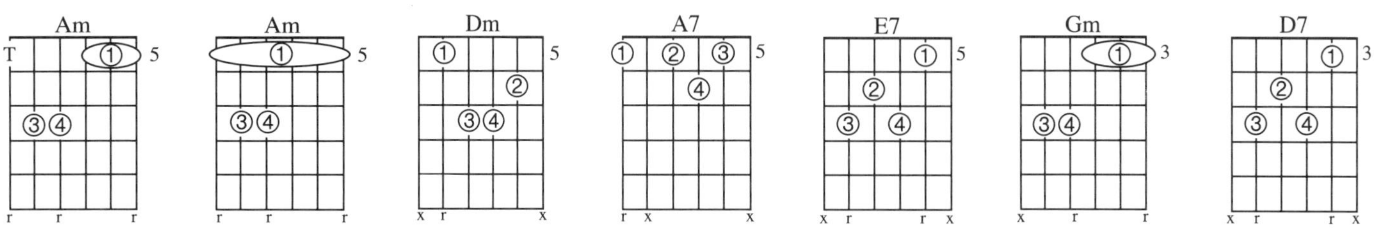

Swing in Minor

Key of Am, CD tracks 18-20

Dix Bruce, 2007

Swing in Minor moved to Dm

Chicago

"Chicago" has been a jazz standard since it was introduced in the early 1920s. It was written by the great Fred Fisher, who also wrote "Peg o' My Heart," "Dardanella," "Daddy, You've Been a Mother to Me," and "Your Feet's Too Big." "Chicago" has a slightly unusual form where only the first four measures are repeated. The melody is built around a repetitive syncopated rhythmic riff. You'll hear it again and again with the lyrics "Chi-ca-go, Chi-ca-go." As you work through the melody, try to get that same swing and bounce. Play it like you'd sing it. You'll notice that I significantly "swingified" the fast version of the melody on the CD. The rhythm just seemed to demand it!

I use the fourth finger quite a bit in playing this melody. As with any melody, you have other choices on the guitar. Try moving the melody up to a different position in the same octave. Here's the first line to get you started.

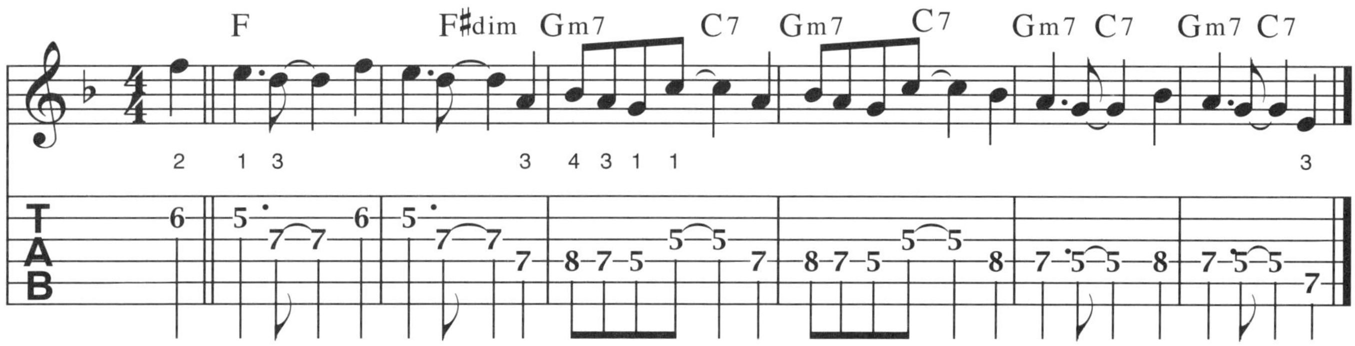

We added a break in the rhythm after the first chorus. Jason plays a rhythm click during the break to keep the band honest, rhythm-wise. In a real life band situation, probably only the soloist would be playing here. You need to keep the rhythm in your head and come in at the right time at the top of the next chorus.

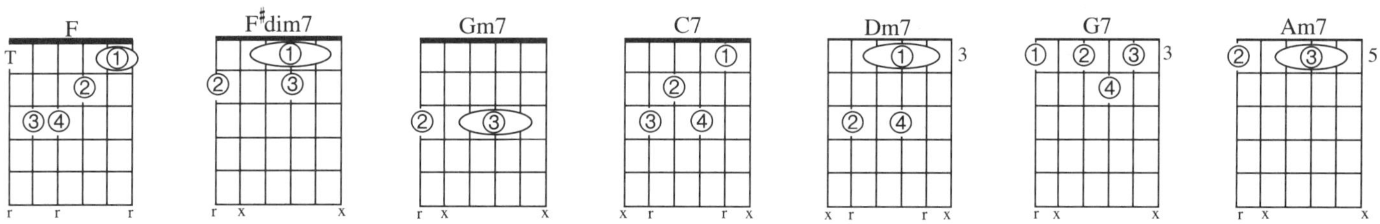

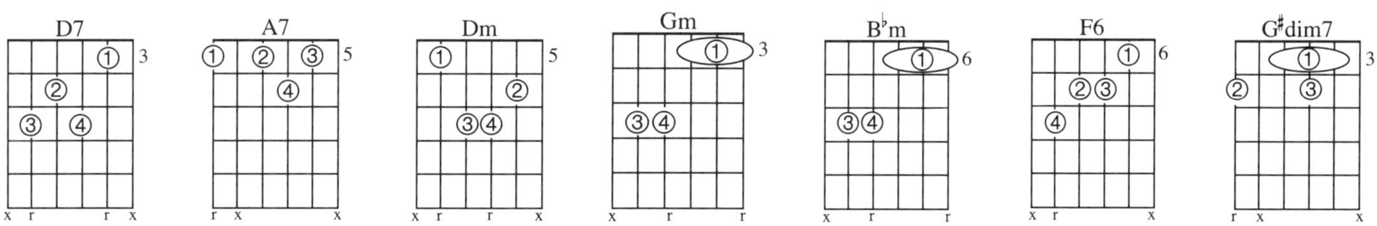

Chicago

Key of F, CD tracks 21-23 — *F. Fisher, 1922*

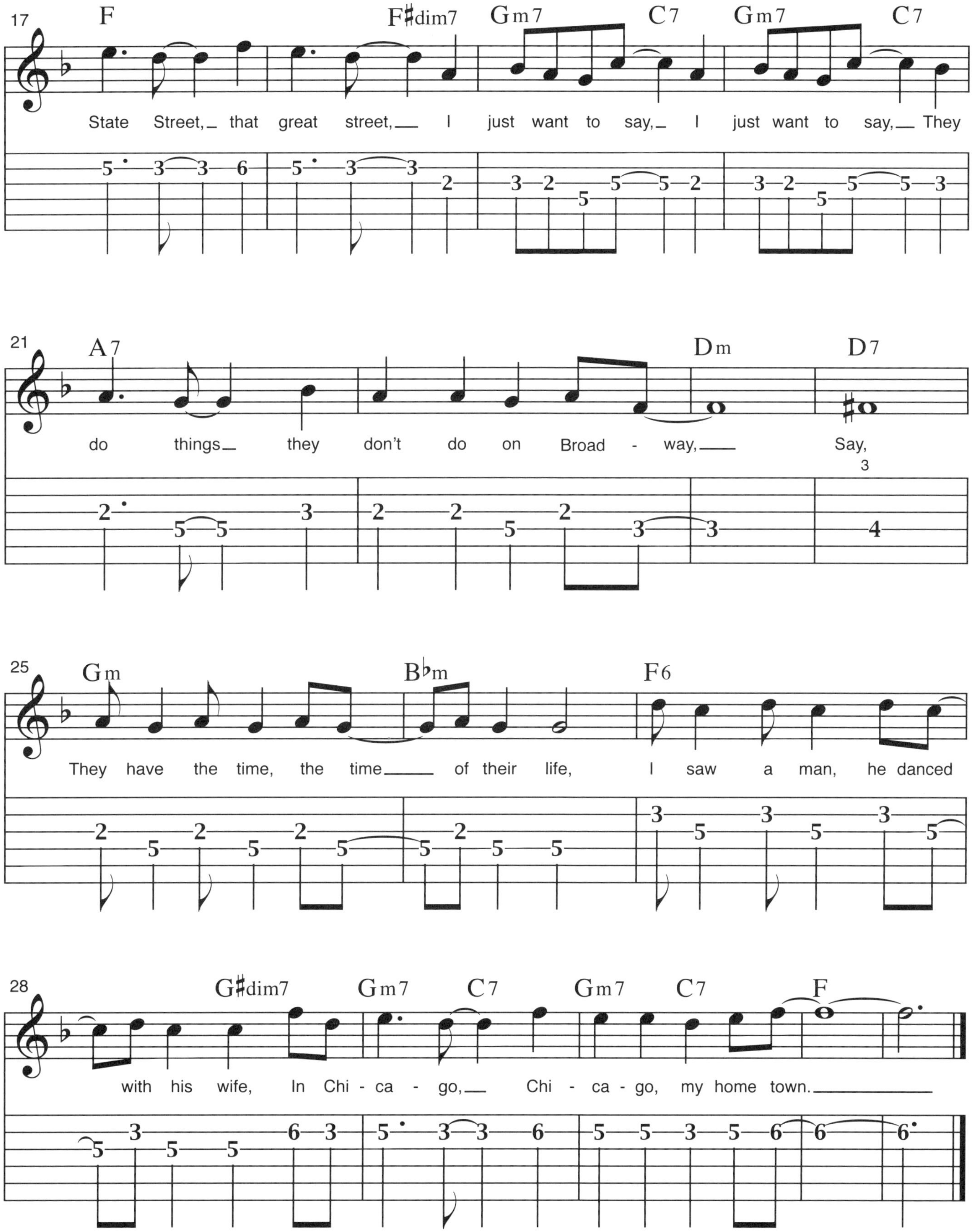
17
F F♯dim7 Gm7 C7 Gm7 C7
State Street, that great street, I just want to say, I just want to say, They
21
A7 Dm D7
do things they don't do on Broad - way, Say,
25
Gm B♭m F6
They have the time, the time of their life, I saw a man, he danced
28
G♯dim7 Gm7 C7 Gm7 C7 F
with his wife, In Chi - ca - go, Chi - ca - go, my home town.

China Boy

"China Boy" has a relatively simple and straight forward legato melody with long, flowing, smooth notes. It starts out in the key of F but modulates to the key of Ab in measure sixteen with the Eb7 chord, which is the V chord of the new key of Ab. The song stays in Ab until measure twenty four where the C7 chord, the V chord of the original key of F, moves it back to the key of F. The modulations give the song an interesting ebb and flow.

On the track I play the melody very close to the way it's written with some syncopations and anticipations to swing it up a bit. Remember: you don't want to play these melodies exactly as written. Be sure to add your own swing and jazz phrasing. If you're not sure what this means, spend some time listening to Django and Stephane and compare what they do to the written versions of these songs.

Since the melody to "China Boy" has lots of longer notes, this is a good one to try playing with octaves. Review the info on octaves on page 20. For this melody we'll need to move up the fingerboard to get better note placement. I've included the first line below to get you started. I use the first and fourth fingers to make all the octaves. Some players prefer to use the first and third fingers on octaves played on strings three and five and four and six. Either way, your fretting hand will jump around quite a bit. Experiment to find octaves that require the least movement. Listen to how effortlessly players like Django and Charlie Christian play octaves.

At about 2:04 into the band track I do a little extra rhythm riff. You can do things like this when you have a second player holding down the rhythm like Jason Vanderford does. I picked a riff that fit with what Jason and Steve Hanson were playing and worked it again and again through the changes and up to the modulation where I reverted to regular rhythm. Then I went back to the rhythm riff for the last eight measures of the key of F part.

The F "barre" form shown below left can be used in place of the Ab form, which uses the thumb to play the sixth string root note. They're pretty much the same form: one with the the thumb, one the barre.

The ending to the track has another typical Django-esque windup and abrupt ending. They're fun to do, they wake up the audience and the band and leave no doubt as to where the song ends.

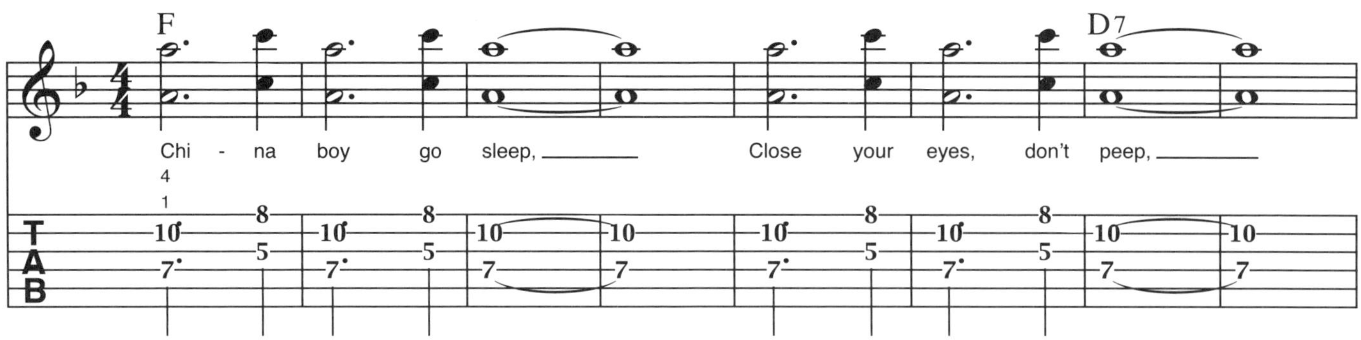

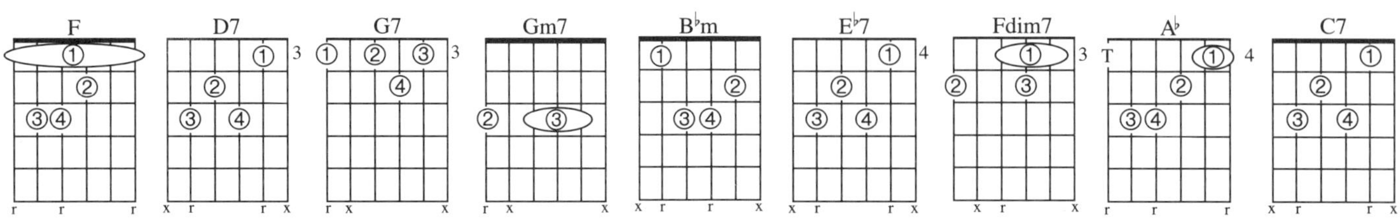

China Boy

Key of F, CD tracks 24-26 *D. Winfree & P. Boutelje 1922*

St. Louis Blues

"St. Louis Blues" was written by W.C. Handy in 1914 and was one of the first blues compositions to become a huge international hit. It's been a standard of jazz musicians all over the world for almost one hundred years and is still played everywhere. Handy also wrote "Memphis Blues," "Yellow Dog Blues," and "Beale Street Blues," among others.

Blues has been called the father of jazz and if you want to understand jazz you need to be familiar with the blues. The blues form is relatively simple and built on a twelve measure pattern: one measure of the I chord (in this case G), one of the IV (C), two of the I (G or G7), two of the IV (C or C7), two of the I, two of the V (D7), two of I. Not every blues has these exact chords in this exact order. Often you'll encounter variations. One of the interesting things about "St. Louis Blues" is that it combines a blues progression with a sixteen measure bridge in a Latin rhythm. It's usually referred to as a tango but some people call it an *habanera*. This part is only played once, during the initial statement of the melody, sandwiched between two sets of blues chord changes. The solos are played over the twelve bar blues chord changes.

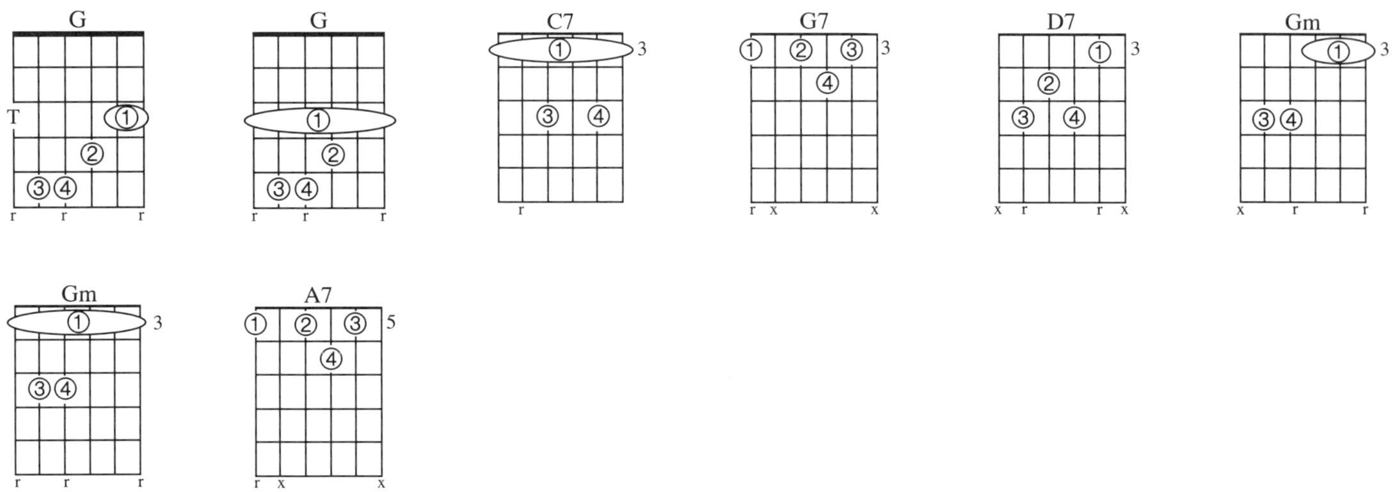

If you're interested in transcriptions of Django's recorded solos see "The Music of Django Reinhardt: Forty Four Classic Solos by the Legandary Guitarist with Complete Analysis" by Stan Ayeroff. It includes transcriptions of Django solos on most of the tunes in this book. For transcriptions with guitar tablature of Django's original compositions, including "Swing 42," "Minor Swing," "Nuages," and many more, see "Complete Django: The Ultimate Django Book" by Max Robin and Jean-Phillipe Watremez. Both are available through the Musix website: www.musixnow.com. Violinists will enjoy a book/2CD set that Jeremy Cohen and I wrote titled "Swing Jazz Violin with Hot Club Rhythm." (String Letter Publishing) It includes all twelve of the songs from this book arranged for violin, plus four additional titles and two jazz string quartet arrangements. Jeremy also wrote and recorded solos to all the songs and included informative instruction on playing violin in the jazz and Gypsy Swing style. It's available from my website: www.musixnow.com. Many of Stephane Grappelli's recorded solos are transcribed in Matt Glazer's book "Jazz Violin."

One of the keys to making your solos sound bluesy is to add "blue notes" to them. The blue notes I use most often are the flatted third and the flatted seventh tones of the scale. For "St. Louis Blues" in the key of G these blue notes would be Bb and F natural. See the scales below.

G major scale

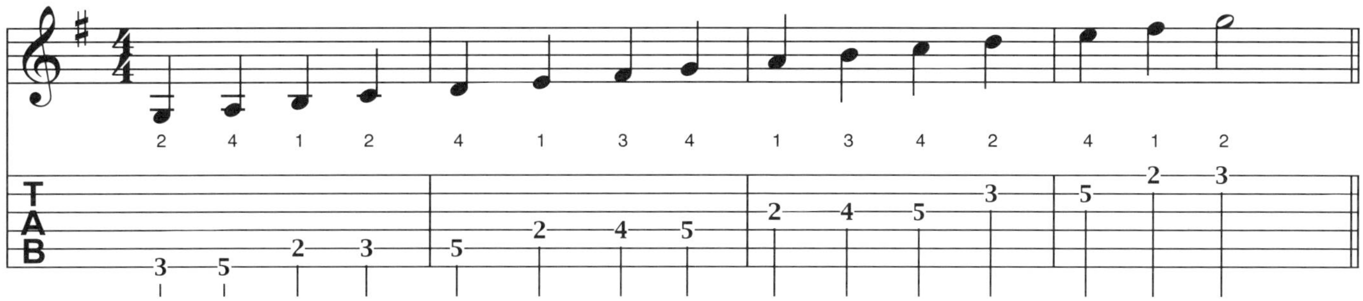

G major scale with blue notes: flatted third and seventh notes

All music has a home tonality and a lot of the interest in a melody or solo comes from moving away and coming back to this tonality or "home." Blues notes provide tension as they work against the home tonality. Once you set up a tonality, your ear expects to hear the regular third and seventh tones. In the case of "St. Louis Blues" in the key of G major, those notes are B and F#. When you add the Bb and F natural notes, it's somewhat unexpected and interesting. Try adding the Bb and F natural tones to your solos. Make sure they reference the root of your home tone, in this case G, and resolve or come back to that tone.

The bridge in Gm is a whole different animal. Here you can use most of the notes of the G major scale with the flatted third and seventh tones, but you most certainly want to avoid or use very sparingly the notes B natural and F#. They're not part of the Gm scale. They would definitely add tension but not quite the right kind for blues. I suggest you stick to the Gm scale for soloing on the bridge.

G minor scale

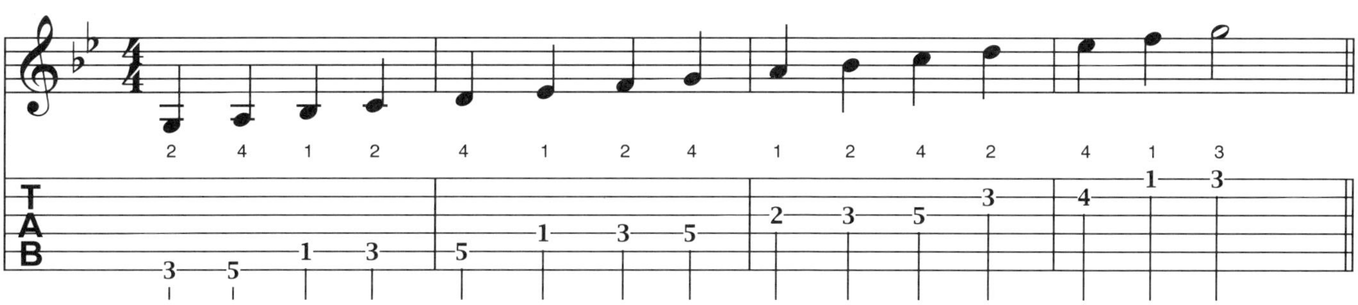

St. Louis Blues

Key of G, Gm, CD tracks 27-29

W.C. Handy, 1914

17
D7
Pulls that man a-round by her a-pron strings.
The man I love would not gone no-where,
21
Gm
Gm A7 D7
no - where. Got the
25
G C7 G G7
St. Lou-is Blues, Just as blue as I can be, That
29
C7 G
man's got a heart like a rock cast in the sea, Or
33
D7 G
else he wouldn't have gone so far from me.

Rose Room

"Rose Room" dates back to 1914 and was a popular song that became an early jazz standard. Duke Ellington's "In a Mellow Tone" uses the same chord changes.

If you find the key of Ab difficult, it's probably because you haven't played in this key much. It's important that you be able to play in all keys. You just never know when a singer might feel most comfortable in a key that's unfamiliar to you. Keep in mind that a singer has a set range and can't stretch it up or down much. With a little bit of work, you, as a guitarist, can transpose any song to any key.

Jason Vanderford plays a simple four bar introduction that lands on the Eb7 or V chord of the key of Ab. You can clearly hear his comping style here — more rhythmic than harmonic — and he plays like this throughout the whole session. He reduces the sound of his chord to where it's barely more than a click. Like many of the Gypsy Swing players he uses a very thick pick that I'd guess is over an 1/8 inch thick. He's acting as a drummer and concentrating on the back beat.

It is typical in Hot Club-style rhythm sections to have more than one rhythm guitarist comping all the time. Django and Stephane usually had two rhythm guitarists in addition to Django. Listen to how beautifully they work together. With multiple rhythm guitarists there can be a danger of actually diluting the groove if all the musicians aren't completely together. Everyone has to be playing the same type of rhythm at the same time and it helps for each player to pull back a bit and serve the band's groove and the soloist, not the ego. In these cases less is more. As you can hear, Jason is a wonderful player because he listens and plays to the groove.

In measures seven through ten the chord progression moves from Db to Dbm, or from IV ("four") to iv ("four minor"). Some players change to the Dbm in measure nine. In this version we change to the Dbm in measure ten. At the end of the first chorus, the band breaks on the first beat of the last two Ab measures. Again, I keep a rhythmic click going so we don't lose the groove. This type of break gives the first soloist an extra two bars to launch into and set up the solo. Breaks like these after the first chorus or melody are prevalent in all styles of swing and jazz.

I recently played a gig where the band performed "Rose Room" as a tango. Give it a try!

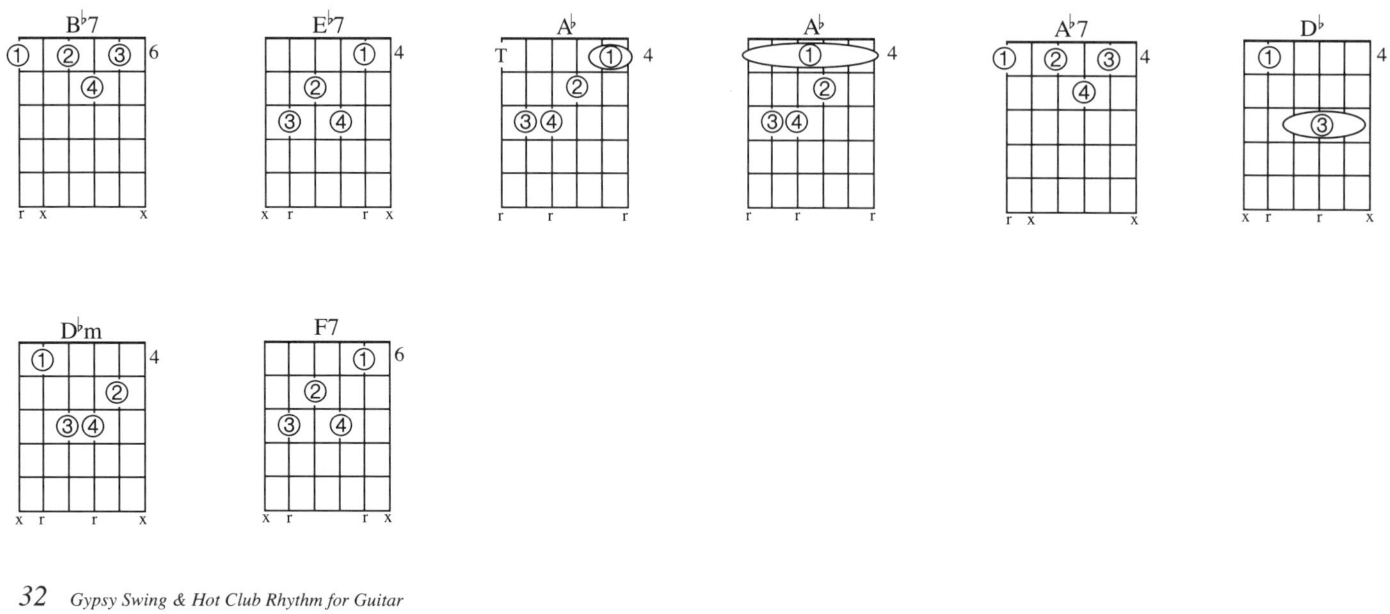

Rose Room

Key of Ab, CD tracks 30-32

A. Hickman & H. Williams, 1917

Arrangement © 2007 by Dix Bruce • www.musixnow.com

Dark Eyes

"Dark Eyes" is probably Russian in origin, certainly Eastern European, and it's one of those songs that evokes wagons around a campfire, dancing and singing late into the night in a gypsy camp. It's loaded with potential for emotion and passion. Our version begins in 3/4 (page 35) and moves into 4/4 (page 36) with a six measure transition. The transition begins with four measures of guitar rhythm, shown below, to set up the new meter and tempo. This is followed with a two measure solo bass fill by Steve Hanson. Solos can be played over either meter, but they're usually played over the 4/4 section, as we've done here. The lyrics are transliterated from the Russian.

Transition chords:

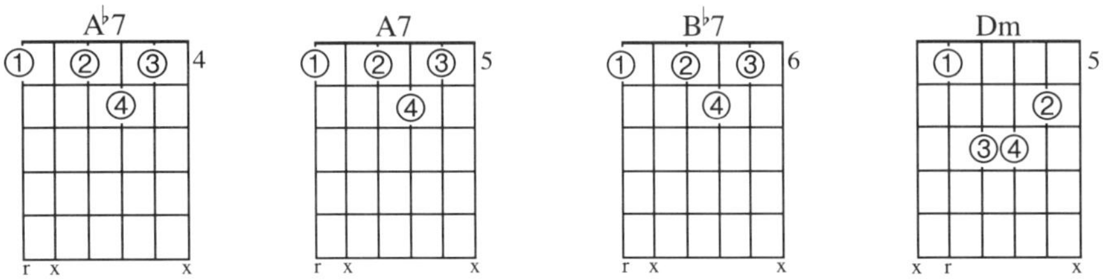

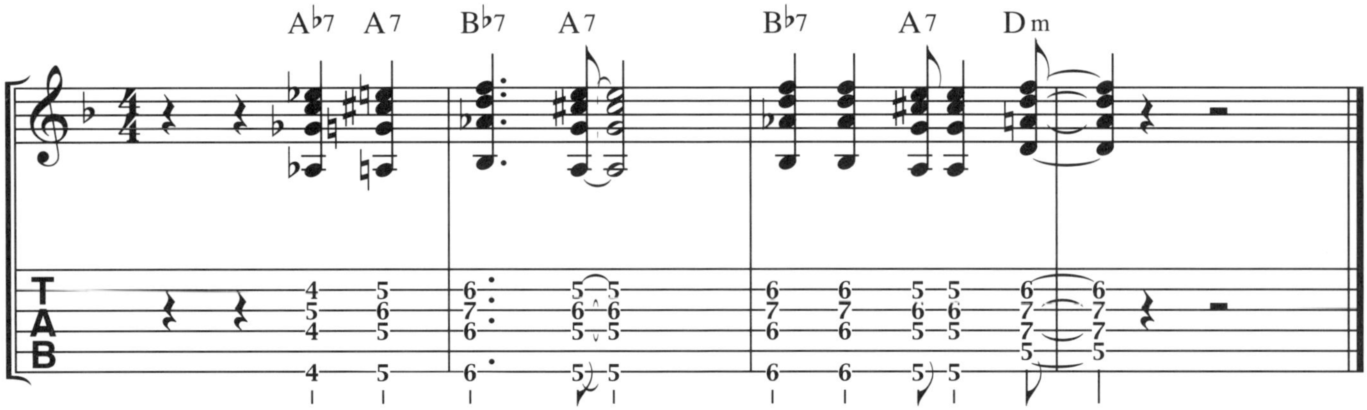

The ending to "Dark Eyes" has a repeat of the final four measures with a *ritard* or slow down on the repeat. If you decide to use this type of ending be sure to warn your fellow players to expect such a thing. If you're the band leader, give clues that something unexpected is about to happen and lead the change in rhythm.

"Dark Eyes" chords:

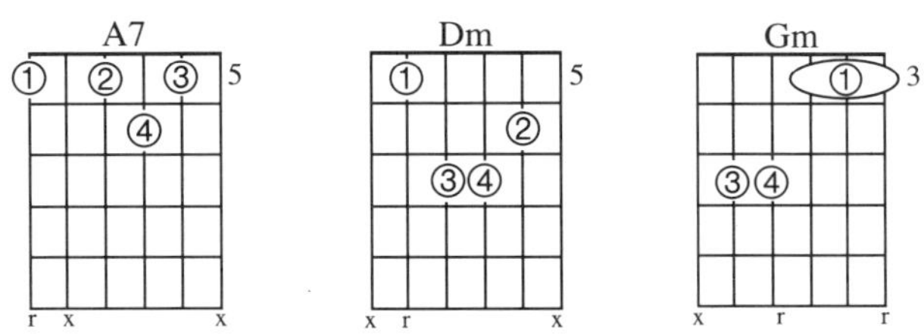

Dark Eyes

Key of Dm, 3/4 time, CD tracks 33-35 | *Traditional, Russian*

Dark Eyes

Key of Dm, 4/4 time, CD tracks 33-35

Traditional, Russian

Swingin' Like '42

"Swingin' Like '42" is based on a popular Reinhardt and Grappelli composition called "Swing 42." They also recorded different tunes titled "Swing 39" and "Swing 48." Generically speaking, "Swingin' Like '42" has what are called "rhythm changes." These are chord changes based on the 1930 George and Ira Gershwin song "I Got Rhythm" and literally thousands of other songs have these same changes. The classic chord changes are I ("one" C), vi ("six" Am), ii ("two" Dm), V ("five" G7), over and over again. Next to blues changes, "rhythm" changes are probably the second most popular in jazz. Musicians often identify a song as "rhythm changes in C" or "rhythm changes in Ab." "Swingin' Like '42," which is in the key of C, has some additional changes and substitutions (minor seven chords for the regular minor chords) but the basic is still considered "rhythm changes" or variations of I vi ii V. "Swingin' Like '42" modulates from the key of C to the key of E and back and uses the same progression I ("one" E), vi ("six" C#m), ii ("two" F#m), V ("five" B7) in the key of E.

In the mid-1970s mandolinist and "dawg" music creator David Grisman often played "Swing 42" in his early Quintets. This popularized the tune among acoustic string jazz and bluegrass players and it became a kind of standard in those genres. The melody to "Swingin' Like '42" will work as a solo on the changes to "Swing '42."

If you play "Swingin' Like '42" more than once through, use the chord changes from the first ending for the last two measures. These changes (C, C#dim7, Dm7, G7) will bring you back to the top of the form. Use the changes as written in the last two measures when you end the song the last time.

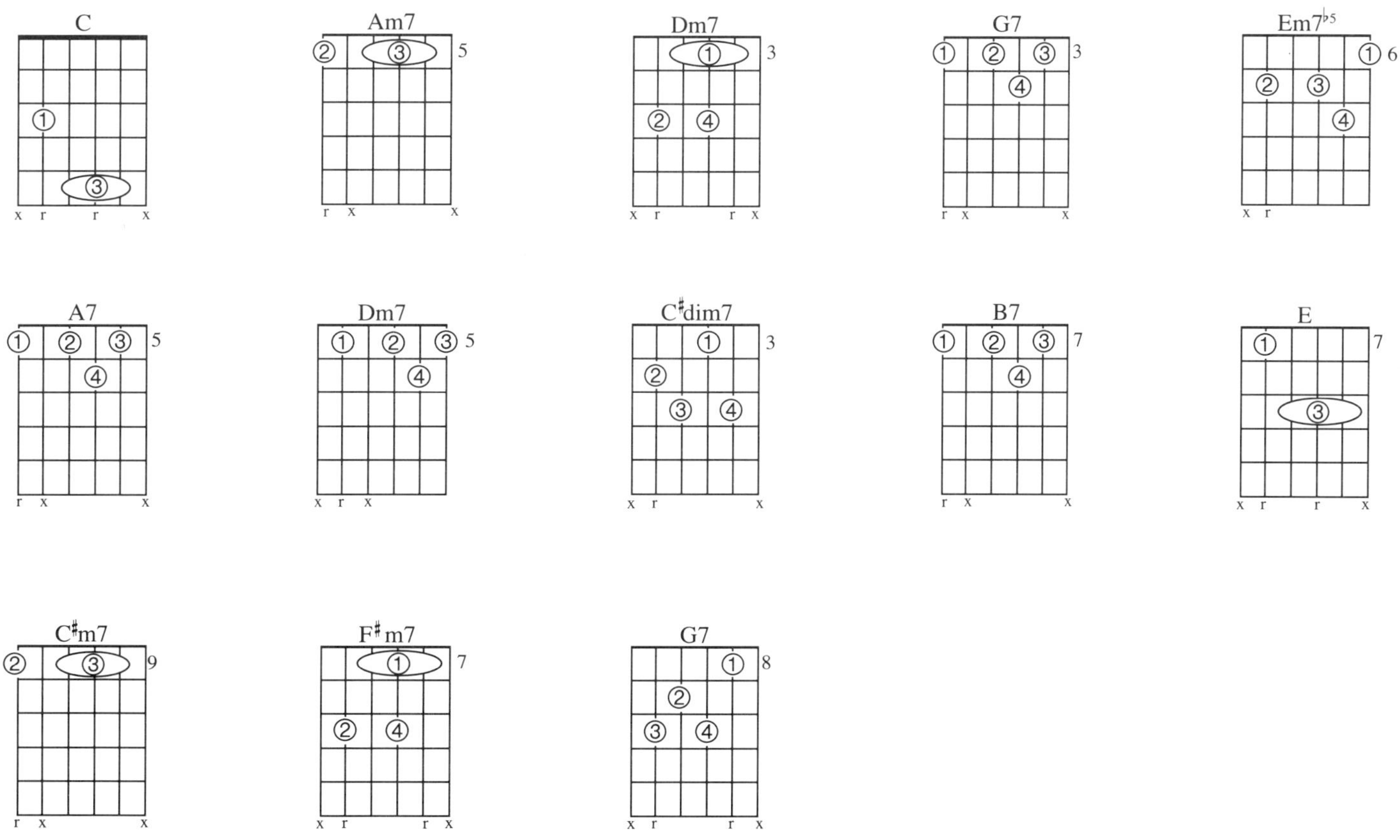

Swingin' Like '42

Key of C, CD tracks 36-38

Dix Bruce, 2007

11
E C♯m7 F♯m7 B7 E C♯m7 F♯m7 B7
15
E C♯m7 F♯m7 B7 E G7
19
C Am7 Dm7 G7 C Am7 Dm7 G7
23
Em7b5 A7 Dm7 G7 C

CD Contents

1. Tuning *(1:02)*
2. The Gypsy Swing rhythm comp *(2:04)*
3. Avalon melody slow *(1:14)*
4. Avalon melody up-to-speed *(:39)*
5. Avalon band track *(3:37)*
6. The Sheik of Araby melody slow *(1:17)*
7. The Sheik of Araby melody up to speed *(:43)*
8. The Sheik of Araby track *(3:06)*
9. Some of These Days melody slow *(1:33)*
10. Some of These Days melody up to speed *(:49)*
11. Some of These Days track *(3:36)*
12. After You've Gone melody slow *(1:21)*
13. After You've Gone melody up to speed *(:44)*
14. After You've Gone track *(3:17)*
15. Baby Won't You Please Come Home? melody slow *(1:16)*
16. Baby Won't You Please Come Home? melody up to speed *(:43)*
17. Baby Won't You Please Come Home? track *(4:15)*
18. Swing in Minor melody slow *(1:17)*
19. Swing in Minor melody up to speed *(:50)*
20. Swing in Minor track *(3:04)*
21. Chicago melody slow *(1:20)*
22. Chicago melody up to speed *(:47)*
23. Chicago track *(4:08)*
24. China Boy melody slow *(:57)*
25. China Boy melody up to speed *(:37)*
26. China Boy track *(3:34)*
27. St. Louis Blues melody slow *(2:58)*
28. St. Louis Blues melody up to speed *(1:50)*
29. St. Louis Blues track *(3:29)*
30. Rose Room melody slow *(1:27)*
31. Rose Room melody up to speed *(:51)*
32. Rose Room track *(4:11)*
33. Dark Eyes melody slow *(1:30)*
34. Dark Eyes melody up to speed *(:52)*
35. Dark Eyes track *(3:57)*
36. Swingin' Like '42 melody slow *(1:27)*
37. Swingin' Like '42 melody up to speed *(:47)*
38. Swingin' Like '42 track *(4:04)*

Index